NURSING SHIFTS AND
RELATIONSHIP DRIFTS:
FINDING HARMONY

Teko Irène Da-Silveira

Table of Contents

Personal Notes

_____

_____

_____

_____

_____

_____

_____

_____

_____

_____

_____

This book is dedicated to my amazing husband who God used to bless me with a life that I never imagined I would be living!

To my family, who is always there to cheer me on regardless of the circumstances!

Personal Notes

_____

_____

_____

_____

_____

_____

_____

_____

_____

_____

_____

_____

Introduction

September 2, 2009 7:30 a.m., a beautiful sunny Wednesday morning. The second I exited the train station on to the fast paced, crowded streets of downtown Chicago, I was greeted by a mildly cool and gentle breeze from Lake Michigan. Five minutes later, as I continued my commute, I heard a man's voice behind me complementing the weather and how he just got back from Miami and loves traveling around the world. Now, if you are anything like me, you probably don't like it when people brag to get your attention (laughing out loud). Despite this, the previous version of me would have been excited to participate in this conversation but, I had my own conversation with God ten minutes prior to getting off that train. The conversation went a little like this, "…dear God, I want nothing to do with any man at this moment in my life. All I want is to focus on my education and excel in it." Boy oh boy, did He have other plans for me! As a first-generation immigrant student, I was on a mission to obtain a degree in graphic design and was fully prepared not to let anything or anyone prevent me from accomplishing this goal. Little did I know that God was placing the right person in my path that would help me get to where I prayed He would position me. I lived in a large city called Aurora, Illinois which is about a thirty minutes drive from Naperville, Illinois. It's funny how we both did the same commute for almost two years on that very same train without ever running into each other until that fortunate day. A simple conversation turned into the exchange of numbers, to meeting at the park that same day for lunch and here we are fourteen years later.

I prayed to God to bless me with a man that would love me unconditionally, guide me, protect me, and show me the world. I'm here to testify that God does not sleep because he answered my prayers. I know you are probably wondering how I went from majoring in graphic design to healthcare. Again, His timing is always perfect. The Great Recession of 2008 to 2009 was the worst economic downturn in the U.S. since the Great depression. This attributed to a decline in domestic products of 4.3%, while unemployment rates doubled to more than 10%, home prices fell by roughly 30% and to top it all, the S&P 500 was down 57% from its highs. It was obvious to me that I needed a plan B. But of course, I was not in the right frame of mind at the time to see things clearly. My boyfriend, who is now my husband, suggested that

I look into a career that offers diversity and job security. The passion that I have for art had to be put on hold temporarily. But before embarking on my journey of becoming a nurse, I had to get out of my comfort zone. In other words, I had to leave the nest to fully spread my wings and I've been doing so ever since. My journey from Illinois to Atlanta began in the summer of 2014, a year after my husband moved to Atlanta. I packed two suitcases and flew to a state that me and my husband have now called home for 13 years. This is where my career journey to becoming a registered nurse began, before eventually becoming a travel nurse in October of 2019.

I would like to welcome you to my nursing shifts and marriage drifts. Whether you are trying to manage the challenges of your nursing shifts or navigate the complexities of relationships, I hope this book will provide you with guidance and advice on how to engage in meaningful conversations in both the workplace and your personal relationships.

Personal Notes

Chapter 1:

POPULAR DEBATE: IS LIVING TOGETHER BEFORE MARRIAGE GOOD OR BAD?

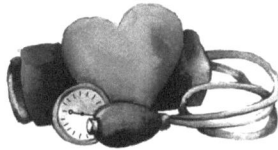

Now before getting into my nursing journey, I would like to share my personal experience with you when it comes to cohabitating before marriage. From my experience, living together prior to marriage gave me the room to learn how to handle problems; both personally and professionally, and how to deal with misunderstandings through communication. Living together before marriage refers to the practice of two individuals in a romantic relationship choosing to share a residence and live together before getting married. This practice has become increasingly common in many cultures around the world over the past few decades. It's a decision that carries both benefits and potential challenges, and people's perspectives on the topic can vary based on their cultural, religious, and personal beliefs.

According to Bribes, there was once a time where living with your significant other before getting married was extremely taboo. This is the opposite nowadays; saying "I do" prior to living together as a couple is now considered a taboo. Per the National Center for Family and Marriage Research, the percentage of women who lived with their partner prior to their first marriage jumped from 11 percent in the mid 1960s to almost 70 percent in 2013. Most people prefer living together with their significant other as a way of exploring whether they can co-exist in a shared space and have a sustaining relationship that will last a lifetime (Lawson, 2022).

To be honest, I pretty much moved in blind without having a clear plan of the outcome of doing so. I truly believe that the trust I have in God to guide my footsteps and to create a clean heart in me guided my decision to pack my entire life into two suitcases and move to Atlanta. Growing up in an African household, this was unacceptable in the African culture but I was not afraid to defy all the odds and follow my heart. Living together for eight years prior to getting married came with benefits and challenges. Ah, before I forget, I should mention that this was my first-time cohabitating with anyone outside of my family. To be honest with you, this decision did not come with its own challenges. Culturally, this decision was frowned upon, which lead to pressure and conflict from social circles and family. The lack of formal commitment prior to me moving in led to my feelings of uncertainty and insecurity but I still trusted the plans that God had for me and I therefore had to trust the process as well. It is imperative to remember that regardless of the noises around you when it comes to what you should or should not do, only you will live with the consequences of your decisions. I made the move because we both believed in this relationship and it was our responsibility to make it work; not the unpopular opinions of your family or friends.

Moving in with him was the best decision of my life! Living together provided me with the insight into how compatible we were as a couple when it comes to sharing living spaces, responsibilities, and day-to-day routines. We had the opportunity to experience each other's habits (the good and the bad), preferences, and quirks in a way that the first two years of dating did not reveal. Cohabiting helped us better understand each other's communication styles, conflict resolutions skills, and overall relationship dynamics. My communication style evolved from holding everything in and going to bed angry to learning how to express my emotions in an effective way that gives him the opportunity to apologize genuinely. You see, I grew up in an environment where a lack of communication was considered normal. Expressing your emotions in a relationship or marriage was frowned upon or considered disobedient. I entered this relationship thinking it was normal not to express your emotions but rather to keep them to yourself, not knowing that doing so would silently kill me. Financially speaking, sharing living expenses proved to be extremely beneficial, it allowed us to get a sense of how we handle financial matters together. I quickly realized early on that I lacked the ability to budget properly and would spend impulsively. Living together deepened our emotional intimacy and reinforced our commitment to the relationship.

That said, and I cannot stress this enough, it is important to note that there is no one-size-fits-all answer to whether living together before marriage is a good idea. I strongly recommend that you consider your own values, beliefs, and circumstances when making this decision. Communication, mutual understanding, and shared goals are crucial regardless of whether you and you partner chooses to cohabit before marriage or not.

Figure 1. Fifty Years of Change in the Share of Women (19-44) Cohabiting Prior to 1st Marriage, by Marriage Cohort

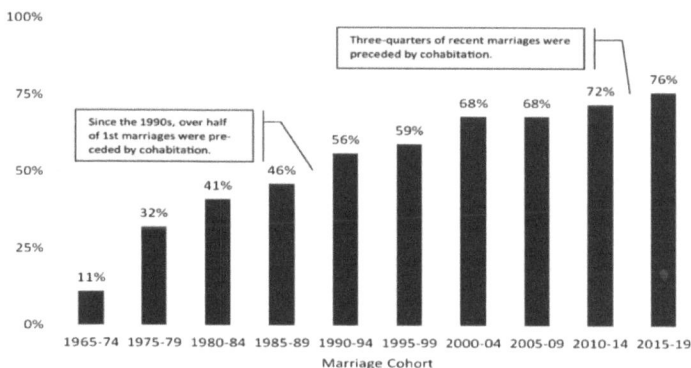

Source: 1987 NSFH (Bumpass & Sweet, 1989); 1995 NSFG (Bumpass & Lu, 2000); NCFMR analyses of female data files from NSFG cycles 2002, 2006-10, 2011-15, and 2015-2019.

Three-quarters (76%) of recent marriages (2015-2019) were preceded by cohabitation.

https://www.bgsu.edu/ncfmr/resources/data/family-profiles/manning-carlson-trends-cohabitation-marriage-fp-21-04.html

Personal Notes

_____

_____

_____

_____

_____

_____

_____

_____

_____

_____

_____

Chapter 2:

IN THE HEART OF CRITICAL CARE: A NEW GRAD'S PERSPECTIVE

I can still recall the day I approached the 71 ICU unit manager. It felt like my nerves were shattering the ground with every step I took, as I made my way towards her to inquire about the opportunity of joining her unit as a new graduate ICU nurse (after graduating and passing the NCLEX). To my surprise, she responded with "I've already hired you as nurse." I was thinking to myself *but how?* I never even interviewed for an RN position. According to her, she hired me based on how I interviewed eight months ago for a nursing tech position and she had been really impressed with my work ethic and overall relationship with my team members on the unit. One of the most valuable lessons that I want you to learn from my experience is that you can work in the ICU as a new graduate nurse if you strategically position yourself, then let your hunger for becoming an ICU nurse speak for itself by being your authentic self, and be teachable.

First and foremost, congratulations on starting your journey as a new graduate nurse in the intensive care unit. The ICU can be an intense and demanding environment, but it is also a place where you can learn and grow as a nurse. Honestly speaking, I owe my success in the intensive care unit to my support system, both in and out of the hospital. I would be lying to you if I sat here and said that building a support network in the workplace will come easy. Although my transition from nurse tech to a registered nurse was fairly smooth, my main struggle was being perceived by a few nurses as still being the unit nurse tech and not a nurse. I even had a nurse ounce utter to me, "I'm finding it hard perceiving you as a nurse and not the tech." What can I say, even the highest degree cannot take the ignorance out of certain individuals. Based on my own experience with other new graduate nurses that did not start their journey on the unit as a nurse tech, it was the transition from the classroom to the bedside that was most terrifying for them.

It is imperative that you build a support network in the workplace because doing so can make a significant difference during challenging times. Till this day, I still find myself in awe of how the relationship and rapport I built with everybody on that unit from environmental personnel to nursing tech to doctors, secretary, etc. helped me get through my journey in the ICU as a new graduate nurse.

Trust me when I tell you that your first year as a new ICU nurse is going to be challenging and a steep learning curve due to the application of new nursing skills. The complicated lifesaving equipment and specialized knowledge required by critical care can be overwhelming, and the fear of making a mistake can put extra pressure on a new grad ICU nurse. Personally, I was able to overcome this challenge by developing my critical thinking skills in assessing situations, analyzing data, and making informed decision. Your critical thinking skills will not only improve your confidence levels but most importantly they will help you to embrace your mistakes and learn from them. Making a mistake as a new grad should be embraced instead of frowned upon because that is how we truly learn as humans. If you make a mistake, use it as an opportunity to learn and grow. Seek feedback and understand how to prevent similar errors in the future. Doing this gave me the confidence to communicate and collaborate effectively with other healthcare professionals in providing seamless and safe patient care.

So how exactly did my experience as a new ICU nurse affect my personal life outside the cement walls of the hospital? Well, I'm glad you asked. But before we dive into all of those juicy details, one of the most important lessons I failed to realize at the time is the fact that I was so busy focusing on being the best ICU nurse possible, I ended up neglecting my personal responsibilities as a daughter, a sister, an aunt, and most importantly as a wife. I was so busy fighting for the lives of my patients that I did not realize I was transporting that pain, anger, and frustration into my personal life. "You are not supposed to carry you work home with you" they say, and there I was doing the exact same thing I was told not to. So how exactly was I supposed to separate the two, especially as a new grad nurse? Oh, don't worry this part was not covered in the thousands of chapters that we buried our heads in to earn the title Registered Nurse. We all know how emotionally, physically, and psychologically challenging caring for critically ill patients and their families can get; on top of that during a pandemic, but what we are not prepared for is the trauma that comes with this role. Personally speaking, learning to cope with these emotions is not only an important aspect of your personal growth but also in your interpersonal relationships.

Here is a useful interactive activity on how to deal with high stress environments and the impact they can have on your personal life.

5 TIPS TO MANAGE STRESS PER MAYO CLINIC HEALTH SYSTEM

Guided meditation

https://www.mayoclinic.org/healthy-lifestyle/stress-management/multimedia/meditation/vid-20084741 (Hesler, 2023).

Practice Deep Breathing with audio guides

https://www.mayoclinichealthsystem.org/hometown-health/speaking-of-health/mindfulness-meditation-improve-your-quality-of-life (Hesler, 2023).

Manage social media time

Spending time on social media sites can become stressful, not only by what you might see on them, but also because the time might best be spent enjoying visiting with friends, being outside enjoying the weather or reading a great book. In addition, many people use social media at night, which may worsen sleep due to increased stress at the exact time people are trying to wind down for the evening, resulting in fewer overall hours of quality sleep (Hesler, 2023).

https://www.mayoclinichealthsystem.org/hometown-health/speaking-of-health/5-tips-to-manage-stress

Maintain physical exercise and good nutrition

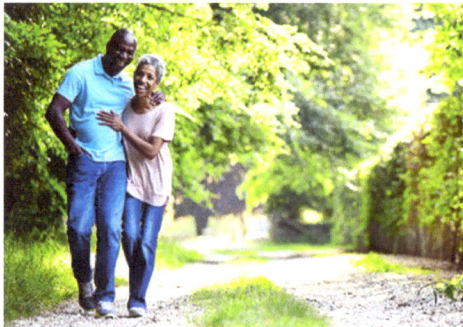

https://www.mayoclinichealthsystem.org/hometown-health/speaking-of-health/establishing-healthy-behaviors-that-stick (Hesler, 2023).

Connect with others

https://www.mayoclinic.org/healthy-lifestyle/adult-health/in-depth/friendships/art-20044860 (Hesler, 2023)

Chapter 3:

THE CHANGE IN CAREER PATH
WAS INEVITABLE!

R emember that embracing change and adapting to new opportunities is a natural part of life's journey. While it may involve some uncertainty and challenges, it also offers the chance to grow, learn, and find a fulfilling path that aligns one's true self. After two years in ICU, I needed a change in my career that would allow me the flexibility needed to focus on self-care and my relationships. I embarked on my journey of fulfillment on October 2019 when I landed in the city of "lost angels", also known as Los Angeles, a week after my honeymoon. After going through a gruesome process of obtaining my California license and credentialing, I embarked on my travel nurse journey. I recall that day in October so vividly, landing at LAX and walking outside to catch the shuttle which would transport me to the designated area for sharerides, with tears rolling down my face I repeatedly asked myself "what are you doing here by yourself?" Isabel Allende said it better that "fear is inevitable, I have to accept that, but I cannot allow it to paralyze me." I would be lying to you if I said the thought of getting back on that plane and going back to my comfort zone did not cross my mind. I made the decision there and then, not to become the hostage of my fear and allow it to dictate what I could and could not do. If you open the door to fear, it will confine you to your comfort zone and deny you of your dreams and aspirations. One thing I know about God is that he will not give you a battle that he is not ready to fight for you. I made the decision to not allow my fears to handcuffed me from taking a leap of faith. Now forgive me for not sharing this little secret of mine with you; I had never lived on my own until now, which explains my thought process and fear during that moment. In life, "it is not where you are going that is fighting you, it is where you left. You have to decide to stay on those old steps to control the noise or are you willing to deal with the noise in order to have the elevation…" (T.D. Jakes).

I bet on myself when I made the decision to deal with the noise that followed my decision of becoming a travel nurse. Now, we all know that the first individuals to frown on the idea of leaving the bedside to go travel or pursue a higher degree are the ones that choose to stay on the old creaky step(s). My decision to embark on this journey could not have come at one of the most unprecedented times; during a worldwide pandemic. My journey began with others questioning my decision to become a travel nurse, and trust me, news travels pretty quickly in the hospital. I heard, "she is chasing money," "she is not loyal," "she is a traitor," "who leaves their husband to chase money," "she should be at home catering to her husband and focusing on making babies." As stated earlier, noises, that is what I called every single one of those comments. Again, it is imperative to know your "why," if not the noises around you will determine it for you.

So, what was my why? Well, I'm glad you asked. First, I didn't only become a nurse to work as a staff indefinitely but most importantly, for personal growth as well. As I evolved and gained new perspectives in the ICU, my interests and passions shifted to exploring how other hospital systems operate in different states, how patient acuity and diagnosis is different across the country, and many more. This led me to pursue different career paths that align better with my values and aspirations. One of my biggest reasons why I pivoted to travel nursing was the lack of a work-life balance. At a first glance, electing to work three 12-hour shifts a week in order to tip the work-life balance scales is very appealing. Imagine for a second the effect of investing four days a week into your personal time, which is 96 hours, 5,760 minutes, and 345,600 seconds, will have on your overall well-being. Well, having four days off per week is appealing at first, but when you work 12, 14, or 16 plus hours in addition to a lengthy commute home, as a nurse it's not really as appealing as it may sound. I recall barely mustering the energy to eat a meal, let alone have time for personal commitments after working a 12 plus hour shift. A four-day weekend might very well allow for more personal time, but as a nurse myself, I was spending that time recovering by sleeping my life away. It was simply not worth it for me.

The first step that I implemented in my journey to achieve a work-life balance was to utilize my skills as a nurse to evaluate my own priorities. For a moment I envisioned myself as the patient laying on one of the 20 ICU beds, fighting for my work and life balance in and out of the hospital. I asked myself the following assessment questions: what would you tell a patient if they were experiencing stress from work-life imbalance? What dimension of your wheel of life have you been neglecting? And the answer to my own question was that I wasn't in an environment that promoted the importance of achieving a work-life balance. So the ball was at my disposal to kick in the direction that I envisioned my life going in. Strategically, I created a personalized care plan that would improve my work-life balance. I invested time into learning all the ins and out of travel nursing and most importantly educated my husband on the journey I was getting ready to embark on. As an executor, not only did I apply for my California license five months prior to the end of my residency program; most importantly, thirteen months into my residency program, I took a leap of faith and took my critical care registered nurse exam to assess my knowledge in the field and to make myself more marketable as an intensive care nurse.

In summary, I like to call this chapter of my life, "do not let anybody's mouth and your own fear stop your feet from moving." If you give others or your fears the power to determine what you should or should not do and when to do it, you might as well authorize he or she to be your warden. Go into the ICU with a plan and execute your plan. Be open to advice and guidance but do not stay within the line that somebody else has drawn for you. Draw your affirmation and your strength from your faith, family, and your circle of close friends. This is advice that I wish somebody had shared with me prior to my journey to the ICU. After all, it is impossible to care for someone who is ill if you are walking around ill yourself.

Personal Notes

Chapter 4:

THE POWER OF A DECISION

The power of a decision cannot be underestimated. The decisions I've made up to now have shaped my life, determined my paths, and influenced my destinies. Every choice I made, no matter how big or small, has positioned me on a particular course of action and lead me to different outcomes. Let's dive a little deeper into some of the key aspects that highlight the power of decisions.

I utilize the power of decision making as my compass to guide me toward my goals and aspirations. When you make a decision that you stand by, it helps you clarify what you want to achieve and sets you on the path to reaching those objectives. The decision to leave my comfort zone to embark on the journey of travel nursing far exceeded my expectations both in the work place and in my personal relationships. Decisions are catalysts for change. Whether it is changing career, starting a relationship, or adopting a healthier lifestyle, every decision has the potential to bring about transformative shifts in our lives.

Working in a new environment surrounded by other nurses with skills from top hospitals instilled this new level of confidence in me that I did not know I possessed. Why? Because in my previous environment, my achievements and improvements used to be frowned upon instead of celebrated. The choices we make often reflect our values and principles. Each decision provides an opportunity to build and demonstrate our character, integrity, and ethical stance. My decision to migrate to an unknown territory thousands of miles away helped me to confront my fears of being surrounded by toxic individuals that crippled my ability to grow in the workplace and step out of my comfort zone. My bold decisions have lead to personal growth and new experiences.

Even if a decision does not lead to the desired outcome, it can still be a valuable learning experience. My decision to travel thousands of miles away didn't exactly have the outcome I had initially anticipated when it came to its effect on my marriage and personal relationships. Because I love to travel and work with a diverse set of individuals, travel nursing was clearly the ideal career for me. However, my journey came with its own unique set of challenges. And one of those challenges was figuring out how to maintain a successful personal relationship along with the challenges of being a travel nurse. It's funny how I used to preach to others that I would never participate in any personal relationship that is long distance. Trust me when I tell you that the power of the tongue is often disregarded. Be careful what you say and how you say it. There is a saying that distance makes the heart grow fonder but I could not help but ask myself, in terms of distance, how far and how long does the heart require to grow fonder? And what happens when the distance is no longer there?

However, I learnt in this journey that distance can also do the opposite; that distance can sometimes be the death knell for many that fail to see the beauty in the chaos. The fact that this was the first time in the eleven years of my relationship with my husband that our marriage had become a long-distance one, I failed to set a realistic expectation on the kind of support that I expected from my husband and what he should expect from me. You might recall that earlier in this book I shared with you how I invested an ample amount of time learning about travel nursing and educating my husband on the journey, I failed to include the subject of healthy expectations in those conversations. And to be fair, realistically speaking, you cannot really set every expectation when it comes to a journey you have never embarked on before. For example, there is a three hour difference between California and Georgia, so imagine the negative impact that this had on our communication. The hectic routine of travel nursing changed my daily, elongated communication or conversations with my husband compared to when I was at home. This lead to misunderstanding, because he did not know what was going on in my life and I did not know what was going on in his. And just like that, the emotional support that I needed to get through the twelve plus hours spent caring for the sickest patients in the hospital was no longer consistently there like it once was.

Initially my beliefs didn't allow me to see the beauty and blessings that this distance could bring into my marriage. This chapter in my life was an eye opener to the fact that I had, until then, failed to appreciate and embrace the little things in my marriage like communicating throughout the day. It is important to recognize that not all decisions will have immediate or obvious effects, and some may take time to unfold. Nevertheless, the power of a decision lies in the fact that it sets us on a particular path and influences the trajectory of our lives. It is crucial to approach decision-making thoughtfully, consider the potential consequences and align the choices we make with our long-term values and objectives. In doing so, we can harness the power of decisions to create a meaningful and fulfilling life journey.

Chapter 5:

EXPOSURE TO OTHER OPTIONS IS THE BEST GIFT

E xposure to other options can indeed be a valuable and transformative gift. Traveling as a nurse gave me the opportunity to explore and learn about different choices, it opened up new perspectives, broadened my horizons, and empowered me to make more informed decisions. Let's now take a look at how beneficial this exposure to other options was and still is to my personal growth.

Being exposed to various options has introduced me to a diverse range of possibilities in various aspects of my life, such as career path, education, travel, hobbies, and relationships. This expanded awareness has helped me see beyond what I was familiar with while encouraging me to consider alternative paths. Once I figured out how travel nursing was affecting my relationship, I immediately considered and embraced the alternative paths when it comes to long-distance relationships that I once frowned upon. The alternative paths exposed me to different options that went on to foster personal growth and development. It challenged me to step out of my comfort zones, try new things and embrace change. This led to increased resilience and adaptability not only in my work life but most importantly, my marriage.

Do not limit yourself by not exploring your options in anything and everything you do. The more we explore, the better equipped we become at making decisions. As a critical care nurse, our job is to think critically by exploring different treatment options for our patients, so I advise that you apply or use the same or similar approach for solving the adversities that we are faced with in our personal lives outside of the hospital. By exploring my options in how to maintain my relationship on the solid rock that God build my marriage on, I was able to gain more insights into the pros and cons of the different choices I was exploring. This enabled me to make well-informed and confident decisions that aligned with the values and goals that my relationship was built on prior to my becoming a registered nurse.

Exposure to diverse options sparks creativity and innovation. By analyzing how I approach various situations that I'm faced with in a twelve plus hour shift, it inspired me to think outside the box and come up with unique solutions to challenge what my relationship was encountering. Learning about my options fostered empathy and understanding. It allowed me to appreciate and respect the perspectives and choices of others, and in this case, respect the perspectives and choices of my husband. I realized that I was so focused on the challenges that come with being a travel nurse and making more money by picking up overtime, working sixteen hour shifts, that I was totally neglecting taking into consideration how my husband felt about his wife being thousands of miles away from home during a pandemic and either too busy at work or too tired to even hold a ten minute conversation with him without falling asleep on the phone. Building empathy for ourselves first and for whatever roadblock we find ourselves in promotes more inclusivity and compassion in our approach when it comes to resolving the problem.

As a new travel nurse, it is very easy to regret leaving the comfort of our staff position and home. By sitting down and carefully exploring the beauty that could come from this journey and the various options that this new chapter could offer me professionally and, in my marriage, I did not regret my decisions at all. The fear of missing out or making the wrong choice diminished when I knew that I had thoroughly considered different possibilities that are within my control. My options helped me to discover more about myself. By trying new things, I uncovered hidden talents, interests, and passions that I did not realize otherwise. Options encouraged me to be open-minded and gave me a willingness to learn from diverse experiences and perspectives.

Life is unpredictable, and circumstances may change. Being aware of different options provided me with the flexibility to adapt to new situations and make adjustments as needed. The quest for knowledge and exploration of various options can become a lifelong pursuit. Embracing continuous learning ensures that we stay curious and engaged with the world around us.

In closing this chapter of my life, exposure to other options has enriched my life, expanded my knowledge, and empowered me to make choices that align with my authentic self. It enabled me to embrace change, embrace new experiences, and lead a more fulfilling life. Whether it is through travel, education, networking, or simply being open to new ideas, the gift of exposure to other options is a valuable and empowering aspect of personal growth and development.

Chapter 6:

DISRUPTION TO MY NORMAL PATTERN

Experiencing disruption to your normal pattern can be both challenging and an opportunity for growth. Whether the disruption is due to unexpected events, deliberate decisions to change, or external factors beyond your control, it can lead to various outcomes and emotions. Here are some insights into how disruption have affected my personal life and relationship.

When my normal pattern was disrupted, it was the most uncomfortable and unsettled feeling. I experienced stress, anxiety, and sometimes confusion as I adjusted to my new changes. My adaptability and resilience were greatly challenge by disruptions. But I overcame these disruptions by using them as an opportunity to learn how to cope with uncertainty and change, which are essential life skills. My fresh perspective on life, work, personal goals and relationships prompted me to question old assumptions and consider alternative paths.

While routines can provide stability, they can also lead to monotony and complacency. Disruptions forced me out of my comfort zone and encouraged me to break free from rigid patterns. When faced with disruptions, I had to think creatively to navigate through the challenges; and this stimulated my problem-solving skills and sparked innovation. We'll explore more about my disruptive life in the next chapter. The value of stability and predictability in my life was highlighted by the disruptions. After going through a period of upheaval, I developed a deeper appreciation for the normalcy I once had. This journey gave me the opportunity to discover strengths and capabilities I did not know I possessed. I felt the beauty of the disruptions when I realized that change is a natural part of life and by accepting this reality, I became more adaptable and open to new opportunities. By successfully navigating disruptions I was able to build resilience and confidence. I became better equipped to handle many future challenges.

With a heavy load lifted off my shoulder, disruptions lead me to introspection and a reevaluation of my priorities. They prompted me to focus on what truly matters and to let go of what no longer serves me. Remember that disruptions are a natural part of life, and they present opportunities for growth and learning. While they can be uncomfortable at first, they can also lead to positive outcomes. Embrace the experience with an open mind, seek support from loved ones or professionals if needed, and be patient with yourself as you navigate through the changes. Over time, you may find that disruptions have helped you evolve into a stronger and more adaptable individual.

Personal Notes

_____

_____

_____

_____

_____

_____

_____

_____

_____

_____

_____

_____

Chapter 7:

CREATIVITY THRIVES IN DISRUPTIONS

Absolutely, creativity often thrives in disruptions. Disruptions can shake up our usual routines, challenge our thinking, and push us to explore new possibilities. It is important to note that while disruptions can stimulate creativity, the process of creativity may still be challenging. Creativity often involves overcoming obstacles, dealing with self-doubt, and being open to experimentation. However, when approached with an open mind and a willingness to explore new possibilities, disruptions can be fertile ground for creative ideas to blossom.

This is how creativity flourished in my times of disruption. Disruptions break us away from established norms and traditional ways of doing things. This opens the door for unconventional and innovative ideas to emerge. As a travel nurse, we are what I like to call free spirits; moving from one location to the next, ready or not to embrace new places, cultures, people, and on top of all that, trying to fit in either a new or old romantic interest thousands of miles away. Is sustaining a long-distance relationship possible as a travel nurse? Absolutely! With creativity of course. Per research, long-distance relationships may even be more successful than traditional ones if positive qualities are present. Now don't get me wrong, this is no easy journey to embark on but before you give up on the idea of having a fulfilling career and relationship let's explore how I made it work.

I quickly realized that I had to break away from my relationship norms and traditional ways of doing things. As a woman that loves cooking for her spouse so much that she cannot convince him to even grab a taco bell, how do you fill that void temporarily when your presence is not there? In a way, I kind of blame myself for converting him from fine dining to being addicted to my cooking. Well, I will tell you how I made this transition easier prior to my travel assignment. A few days prior to leaving for my assignment, I food prepped for at least two weeks, and scheduled deliveries of similar meals to what I would cook for him when at home. Now don't get me wrong, it's not that my husband is not able to order these meals for himself or cook, but there is something special about me personally ordering those meals from California to be delivered to him at home and sometimes at work. To make things more interesting, I never share with him what I am ordering, as a way to surprise him. Once the food arrives, we hop on a video call together and enjoy our meals while watching a movie together, just like at home.

When you break away from the norms, it opens the door for unconventional and innovative ideas to emerge. Although I encountered new problems that require creative solutions, adapting to these challenges fosters a climate of innovation. Whether I liked it or not, I was forced to see things from different angles and reconsider my assumptions. This cognitive shift in perspective sparked my creative insights and approaches. Creativity thrives in environments where adaptability and flexibility are valued. Disruptions demand ways of thinking, encouraging creative problem-solving. Sometimes, we are faced with ambiguity and uncertainty, which can be uncomfortable but also lead to breakthroughs as we explore various possibilities. When the usual pattern is disrupted, there is often more freedom to experiment and take risks. This experimentation can lead to creative discoveries. This experience drew my relationship closer to the point where my husband and I brainstorm ideas and share perspectives on how to sustain our love thousands of miles away. Collaboration and collective thinking fuel our creativity. In order to adapt to our new normal, we endured a learning process that triggered creativity as we gathered new knowledge and insights. Disruption challenged the status quo and encouraged us to think beyond conventional boundaries, thus paving the way for innovative solutions.

Various emotions were stirred throughout this journey, creative outlets such as traveling together, him visiting, especially when I was on an assignment by myself, or planning a trip to meet up in another country, or even listening to our favorite playlist together on Spotify became a powerful way to express and process these emotions. This creative outlet offered my relationship opportunities to be reinvented through creative thinking and exploration. The beauty in all of this was that instead of fighting the change and uncertainty, we learned to embrace it, making things more adaptable during times of disruption. Whether it is in art, business, science, or any other field, disruptions can act as catalysts for breakthroughs and innovations. Embracing and harnessing the creative potential in times of disruption can lead to transformative outcomes and help us thrive in the face of change.

Chapter 8:

IN THE MIDDLE OF THE CHAOS, THERE WAS YOU; MY PEACE!

This is dedicated to my loving wife.

What is a husband? As God says, your unconditional acceptance of your wife is not based upon her performance but, on her worth as God's gift to you! If you want your wife to love you unconditionally, always be sure and make it your responsibility to keep her emotional tank full. One of the easiest things to do as a husband is to just allow your wife to wonder, but, as a husband, according to the book of life, you are to lead your wife and be her life support.

Now let's think about my wife who happens to be a travel nurse. I know what you're thinking, I have it easy as a husband because she is not at home for months. She has an extremely lucrative career, I have an enormous amount of freedom and I can do whatever I want in her absence. How far from the truth! You see, my wife worked through the pandemic when it was at its worse. Giving up our life to sustain others (selflessness), millions of individuals perished during COVID-19, and I can only think about how she went to work week after week after week for three years working 13 hour shifts, wearing personal protective equipment and not knowing what the next day would bring. I hope you all understand that she was walking through the fire alone, and it sometimes made me feel helpless but, knowing the grace of God was with us this entire time, she never caught COVID and neither did I. She is my avenger.

So when most people get married, they are usually going to be in the same household together everyday. You are going to see them in the morning, talk to them perhaps during lunch, and then you return home to an evening together. Now let's talk specifically about a traveler nurse marriage. I get up in the morning and my wife is not there. I go to lunch, not able to reach my wife because we are on a different time zone. Now understand this, we live in Atlanta but my wife loves traveling to California to accept assignments. So we are dealing with a three hour time difference. If you are not aware, most assignments are between eight to thirteen weeks. Do you think I'm happy having my wife away from me for that length of time? Now they say you marry for better or for worse, through sickness, and or health, now none of this is healthy for me. As the husband in this marriage, I support my wife's dreams and getting through nursing school was a tall task. The countless nights of studying, all the exams, all the clinicals, residencies, and not to mention the sweat. But knowing all this, it was still our decision that travel nursing was what she wanted to do most. So knowing this, what kind of a man would I be to deny my wife of something she worked so hard to become? These days and nights I am home by myself, but I know for sure it is worth it all. It makes for a celebration when her assignments end and what that means to me is priceless.

However, this journey didn't start out so well. We had just gotten married and returned home from our honeymoon in Egypt. Then, less than seven days later she was headed to her first assignment. Now mind you, me and my wife have been together for eleven years and I had gotten so used to her being by my side day in and day out. She is an ideal wife, she cooks for me, cleans, and comforts me. Now imagine all of that gone?! I depended on her so much that when she left I walked into the kitchen like it was a new room in the house! Do you mean I have to cook now and clean and do laundry? And wait a minute, at night when I go to bed, you mean to tell me there is going to be no one there? And when I get up in the morning, she is still not going to be here?! Oh hell no, she is quitting this! And this was just after a week or two. But, being an understanding husband and respectfully acknowledging that I have the capacity to take care of myself, it helped me to realize how much my wife really meant to me and how much I really depended on her. So, through all of this, the most difficult part has been not being able to hold her at night after she has been through a day of rolling bodies to the morgue. Can you imagine how painful it must have been to know that you were the last person a patient saw who passed away from COVID when family members were not allowed in rooms to support their loved ones? So how can I complain knowing that my wife was trying to save lives and I am at home wondering about cooking chicken on a Thursday!

So the months go by and I realized how much stronger I was getting, and in speaking with her I could hear the strength in her voice as well. I don't know if I mentioned, in between this time there were conversations about her coming home. Not by my choice but by her own, she started to feel home sick, because she was alone. So I said to her "We do not quit in this family and you signed a contract and you need to adhere to it." I consider this being responsible, because as a man, my belief is that you are only as good as your word.

Marriages are challenging to begin with, you have hills and valleys, there are good times bad times, there are of course differences, so no two individuals are going to stay on the same page all of the time. Even in her absence, with her not physically being in the same house, we dealt with this as well. There were countless times when she did not get my point and vice versa. So how do you handle that? I could easily hang up the phone and not answer her calls, but how elementary would that have been. You have to understand that there will be differences. As a married couple, we agreed that we would resolve any negativity in the moment and not let it carry into another day. And yes, we actually do live by this and I have to admit there is no one happier. We're not young and chasing life, instead we are living life together and the maturity in this marriage has always guided us to a safe place together. You see my wife is my best friend (I really do mean this), so there is nothing that we can't share and we don't have secrets. Now don't get it twisted, we have disagreements and while we do not like each other sometimes, we still love each other all of the time.

Here is my advice, if you don't have discipline, don't get married (this is from a man). I support my wife in all her endeavors. She is a part of me that is missed when she is away on assignment, but as a husband it is my responsibility to be an effective communicator and an ear to her communication. As a husband to a travel nurse, I should always show love and support. This is vital. I took on a commitment in a marriage with her and I should fulfill that duty. Being accountable to one another, not policing or parenting each other but promoting a healthy oneness and creating boundaries.

It is crucial to remember that roles and responsibilities in a marriage or relationships in a marriage can be unique to each couple, and they may evolve over time based on the couple's needs and circumstances. "Love knows not distance; it hath no continent; its eyes are for the universe." I believe in the immeasurable power of love; that true love can endure any circumstance and reach across any distance." I love you and miss you when you are away, here is my prayer that I send to my wife everyday. Good morning; hope you are feeling well and being cautious and working smart… Dear father God on this day and every day cometh, help me be strong for her on the days she is feeling weak, and help her be strong for me on the days I am feeling weak, and Lord, please give us both strength for all that's ahead. Help us to NEVER lose faith in you or give up on each other. Thank you Lord, for my amazing wife.

Chapter 9:

FINDING BALANCE IN THE DISRUPTION

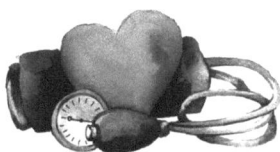

Finding balance in the midst of disruption is essential for maintaining well-being, making sound decisions, and effectively navigating through challenging times. I found my balance by first taking time to understand my emotions, thoughts, and reaction to the disruption. Practicing mindfulness and self-reflection allowed me to gain clarity on how my situation was affecting me. I once neglected self-care, but in this case, I was forced to make self-care a priority. This included getting enough sleep, staying physically active by joining a pilates class, and engaging in activities that brought me joy and relaxation, as well as being grateful for every second that I have an opportunity to talk to my husband. It is easy to feel overwhelmed and stretched thin, and boy I was. I had to learn to say no to additional commitments that contributed or would contribute to increasing my stress. I was once told that I need to develop a clear distinction between my personal and professional life. What this advice failed to take into consideration is how to do so in the specific line of work that I'm in. I learned how imperative it is to lean on friends and family for support and feel safe enough to share certain traumatic events that could not be left at the door after doing what we do as healthcare workers. Do not allow anybody to shut you up or down when it comes to sharing something that should be shared in order to relieve an emotional trauma that is affiliated with your feelings. Talking about your feelings and experiences can and will help you process emotions and gain new perspectives.

I created a weekly routine to provide a sense of stability and predictability amidst the disruption. Routines can help to keep you anchored during uncertain times. Setting boundaries on media consumption to reduce stress really is key. Constant exposure to the news and social media while living thousands of miles away from home during a pandemic can add to your anxiety. As my situation evolved, I remained open to adjusting my plans and expectations. I focused on the aspects of the disruption that I could control and work on while letting go of what was beyond my control to avoid unnecessary frustration. Even during challenging times, find things to be grateful for. Cultivating gratitude can shift your focus from negative to positive aspects of your life. Continue to engage in activities that hold significance for you. An activity that hold significance to my marriage is traveling together and exploring the wonders of the world. I did not allow being away from home to interfere with that aspect of my marriage.

Pursuing meaningful hobbies and projects was key in my journey, providing me with a sense of purpose outside of the hospital. I used to tell myself that I was there to work and work only, which was a mistake because nothing and nobody has the power to tell you when to stop living. Chasing after overtime was replaced with being active, making time to sit and have what I called a virtual date and/or date night with my husband, as well as exploring ways to gain my time back. I was deliberate in my decision-making and took into consideration the potential consequences of my choices and how they align with my long-term goals; not working at the bedside indefinitely. Lessons and opportunities for growth from my disruption blessed me with the opportunity to develop new skills and gain valuable experiences. Disruptions can be emotionally draining, so it is important to practice self-compassion. Acknowledge that it's normal to face challenges during such times, and treat yourself with kindness. I would be lying to you if I sat here and said that I did not neglect myself mentally, physically, emotionally, mentally, and spiritually throughout this chapter of my life. Working throughout a three-year pandemic caring for patients and being surrounded by nothing but deaths every day, holding a tablet in your hand in an isolated room by yourself while kids and/or family say their last goodbyes via Zoom, to doing postmortem care, to actually wheeling the deceased to the morgue yourself only to be told that you have a new admission arriving in five minutes, took away a part of my identity and spirit that cannot be restored overnight. And the worse part about this is not being able to share this horrific experience with my husband because to him I should leave work at work.

Finding balance during a disruption is an ongoing process that requires continuous adjustments. I had to be patient with myself and my husband for not understanding my why behind sharing these stories with him as I navigated through the changes. Now remember this, finding your balance in your disruption does not mean eliminating all stress or discomfort; it is about managing and litigating these feelings in a healthy and constructive way. By prioritizing self-care, seeking support, and embracing flexibility, you can better cope with disruptions and maintain a sense of equilibrium in your life.

Chapter 10:

OVERCOMING THE ABSENCE OF INTIMACY

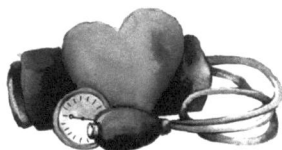

As a travel nurse, being away from loved ones and dealing with the absence of intimacy can be challenging. The absence of intimacy can create loneliness that causes us to overvalue strangers and devaluate people who are the closest to us. As stated by John Caicoppo, University of Chicago psychologist, "loneliness is an aversive signal, much like thirst, hunger or pain" that social media platforms like Facebook, Instagram, and others cannot necessarily curb when it comes to social isolation. Contrary to belief, people that turn to social media have reported feeling lonelier, according to the AARP survey. I am a strong believer in building every relationship on a foundation that is as strong as possible, because you never know how these foundations will play a role in your disruption one day.

The number one foundation that my relationship has been built on for fourteen years, that has helped me cope with the absence of intimacy and find emotional support even when I'm far from home, has been communication. For fourteen years I cannot recall a day in my relationship that I did not communicate with my husband. You see I was the type of person that likes to hold my feelings and frustration inside until they start eating me away. During one of my visits to see him early on in our relationship, I was reminded that I cannot lay in the same bed with him with an angry heart or else I would be free to pack my stuff and go back to my comfort zone. I cannot stress this enough, stay connected with your loved ones through regular communication. It does not matter if it is via video calls, phone calls, or messaging apps - it all counts. Regular communication helped me bridge the distance and maintain emotional closeness. Working over fifty hours a week did not allow me to built a support network with colleagues, fellow nurses, or other healthcare professionals. The communication with my loved ones provided the companionship and a sense of community until I realized that this alone was not sufficient.

Take advantage of your travel nursing assignment by exploring the local area. Engage in activities, join clubs or meetups, and participate in community events. This can help you feel more connected to your temporary home. Focus on self-care to maintain your emotional well-being. Engage in activities that bring you joy, reduce stress, and promote relaxation. Self-care can also help you feel more content and fulfilling during your assignment. As nurses, post a long shift, the last thing we want to do is sit down and write our feelings on a piece of paper. But writing down your thoughts and feelings in a journal, where you express your emotions can be cathartic and help you process the challenges of being away from loved ones. My journal is my husband. From waking up in the morning to when I close my eyes at night, talking to him is my way of writing down my thoughts and feelings because your home will always recenter you when you find yourself lost and frustrated in this world. My home is my husband. I always feel secure and safe, no matter where I am in the world because he does not play when it comes to his wife and his best friend.

In our profession, as nurses and travel nurses, it is easy to immerse ourselves in saving lives and focusing on our career growth. It's also important not to only seek fulfilment and success in our profession but most importantly in our relationship. This is key for maintaining a more balanced and self-assured relationship. Remember how worked up we get when we have an upcoming date? Well, that is how I focus on myself during my assignment because I want to come home to my husband as the irresistible woman he met fourteen years ago. Leave your spouse with a little something that will make him look forward to your presence, your touch, your love and much more when you are not at home. I also implemented mindful meditations in my daily routine to stay present and grounded which helped to reduce feelings of loneliness and anxiety associated with being away from home. While it may not be the same as the intimacy with a romantic partner, meaningful friendships can provide emotional support and a sense of intimacy on a different level.

Remember that being a travel nurse is a temporary arrangement, and it is natural to miss intimacy during this time. Embrace the unique experiences and opportunities that come with travel nursing while staying connected with your loved ones and nurturing your emotional well-being. Over time, you will develop resilience and adapt to the challenges, making your journey as a nurse a rewarding and enriching one.

Chapter 11:

QUALITY TIME: FINDING HARMONY BETWEEN ME AND WE

When we embarked on this journey as a couple, we both had common goals for why we were willing to sacrifice the time apart to achieve these goals. Working toward shared aspirations truly strengthened my marriage. As much as I want to commit to longer contracts to lock in those juicy rates, I had to prioritize my marriage by being mindful in creating a timeline for when the long-distance phase will end and not work at all during my time off. I cannot express enough the importance of open communication and mutual understanding in this journey.

Regardless of where you are on your relationship voyage, relationships are a balancing act. Prior to travel nursing, I asked myself, "how can I pursue my dreams of becoming a travel nurse without neglecting my marriage?" or "can I really have both; a successful career and marriage if I feel like I'm always putting myself last?" Satisfying both individuals as well as relationship growth is a tenacious task for many couples and the disruption of the pandemic made these tasks even tougher. The pandemic redefined the "relationship script" and completely changed how we spend quality time with ourselves and with each other. I learned to constantly adjust to this ever-evolving time because no relationships have been immune since. Understanding the balance of me and we time helped me to fully grasp how to spend a fulfilling and quality time in my relationships. Embarking on this disruptive journey allowed me to explore why my me-time was important for my marriage. On a further level specific to romantic relationships, it was imperative that I felt like an individual within my relationships and to accept the fact that it's ok to nourish my own basic needs. One of the main goals in any relationship is to be close while maintaining an identity as an individual. By celebrating my individuality within my relationship during my travel assignments, I realized that I was happier and more open to intimacy and connection with my husband.

My hope for sharing my journey from new graduate nurse to becoming a travel nurse and how I dealt with the disruption that came with it, is to first let you know that you are not going through this by yourself. Remember that you are not alone in facing disruptions or difficulties, seek support and understanding from your close circle as that can make a significant difference in how we cope and navigate through life's challenges. As stated earlier, there is beauty in every disruption; good or bad. Rather than focusing on the bad, I perceived the challenge as an opportunity to foster self-care in order to be fully present in my relationship. In case you ever find yourself in my position, I would like to share a few pieces of advice with you. Identify activities that assist in bringing you joy. Keeping my me-time sacred gave me something to look forward to. Be open to trying new things that promote positive support and growth that your partner can also incorporate in his routine. Most importantly, be respectful by not imposing your idea of me-time onto your partner. I used to pressure my husband into getting massages with me or getting pedicures with me. I was not mindful of the fact that I was simply imposing what I consider to be self-care on my husband. After that, I instead helped him to understand how self-care positively impacts my health and therefore the health of the relationship as well.

Now what I consider quality time in a relationship may not be exactly what you consider quality time in your relationship; and that is ok. You have to ask yourself, what do I consider to be quality time in my relationship? Is it relaxing or adventurous, or even a combination of both? Although the answer to this question may alter over the course of the relationship, what you define as your quality will help you feel refreshed and connected in your relationship. As nurses, we are faced with so much stress that we do not feel known. There are thousands of published articles highlighting the reasons why some people might choose not to be in a relationship with a nurse. Honestly speaking, the writers behind these articles failed to know nurses. At the end of the day, we are not in a relationship with them. Per study, one of the key elements to a triumphant relationship is to know and feel known by your partner. It is vital to the health of the relationship that both individuals have access to each other's inner world as the relationship evolves and grows over time. I did not allow my career as a travel nurse to alter my love map, rather, I opened the door to this opportunity to organically place its own stamp on my love map through the time allocated to spending quality time together.

Every assignment taught me the true meaning of "make time to make time." I used to underestimate how much my husband values and cherish every second he gets the opportunity to be at home with me until I realized the why behind it. This was his way of communicating "you are important to me," because nothing communicates "you are important to me" than prioritizing time with your spouse to show them how special he or she is to you. I have absolutely no regret of embarking on this journey; it has allowed me to see the beauty in the times when I feel drawn to my husband as well as the times when I feel the need to pull back and replenish my sense of autonomy. If you find yourself in a tug-of-war in your relationship, do not fret. Instead, find resources that will guide you and your partner through discussions on how you can better strike this balance in your relationship.

Personal Notes

_____

_____

_____

_____

_____

_____

_____

_____

_____

_____

_____

Bio

Teko I. Dasilveira was born in Lome, Togo. She migrated from Togo to Benin and from Benin to the United State of America in the year 2000.

She studied graphic design for two and a half years at the American Academy of Art, Chicago and then left to Atlanta, Georgia to continue her education on a different path. In 2008, she graduated Sigma Theta Tau International Honor Society of Nursing from Chamberlain University with a bachelor's degree in nursing.

Her nursing career begin at Emory University Hospital Atlanta as a critical care nurse for three years prior to becoming a travel nurse. After working as a travel nurse for three years at some of the top hospitals in the country, she embarked on the journey of becoming an entrepreneur by obtaining her license as a life and health insurance broker.

Teko is passionate about helping families build generational wealth by protecting their legacy and showing them the right formula to do so, one family at a time.

Besides helping families both in and out of the hospital, Teko loves to travel all over the world with her husband to gain new inspiration and explore the wonders of the world.

RESOURCES THAT GUIDED ME THROUGHOUT MY JOURNEY

Lois Twum

M E N T O R S

Damon Dillard

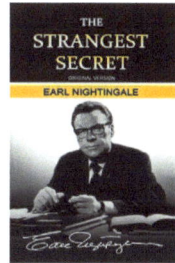

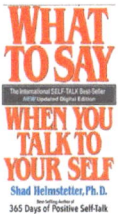

—— Myron Golden

Resources:

https://www.bgsu.edu/ncfmr/resources/data/family-profiles/manning-carlson-trends-cohabitation-marriage-fp-21-04.html

https://www.brides.com/story/living-together-before-marriage-study

https://www.mayoclinichealthsystem.org/hometown-health/speaking-of-health/5-tips-to-manage-stress